MASTER
THE ART OF
catfulness

'WHAT GREATER GIFT THAN THE LOVE OF A CAT.'

CHARLES DICKENS

December 25, 2020

Christmas day, and I got this journal as a gift. My two cats are Ringo and Quincy, and I love them _so_ much. Cats are one of my favorite animals, along with crows, other fat birds, raccoons, and basically anything but dogs. Dogs can go die lmfao. If it weren't for my cats, I'd be dead too, probably. Cats = life Cats are better than people, in fact waaay better. they bury their shit, catch their own meals, and never invade anyone's space (unlike dogs). Dogs slobber all over you, they bark all the time, and they pounce on you for no reason and sniff + lick your coochie. Disgusting, if you ask me. But what's just as bad as dogs are dog people. Dog people are the spawn of evil because they're just TOO NICE. Seriously, they're TOO PEPPY and overly cheerful for _what_? They can rot in hell.

12/25/20

FIX YOUR EYES ON THE PREY AND SLOWLY MOVE TOWARDS IT!

Hunt like a cat and make a list of three goals you want to achieve over the next year.

With each goal write three things you can do to help you move in the direction of success.

1. Be strictly vegetarian and diet healthily. Try to take 15 minute walks after eating and

2.

3.

THE BEST *therapist* HAS FUR AND FOUR LEGS

PRESS PAWS. When you're feeling anxious, massage the centre of each palm with the thumb of the other hand, moving in a circular motion.

'TIME SPENT WITH CATS IS NEVER WASTED.'

SIGMUND FREUD

LIVE IN THE MOMENT. Cats make meditation look easy. They slip into a reflective state in the blink of an eye. Follow their lead and take a moment. Stop, breathe and take everything in. Engage your senses. What can you see, hear, smell, taste and feel?

COURAGE AND CATTINESS

Follow the furry creed and foster self-belief.
Make a list of five things you've achieved so far
this year, even small successes count. Read it
with pride and celebrate your pawesomeness!

1.

2.

3.

4.

5.

CATS
HAVE CLAWS
AND THEY'RE
not afraid
TO USE THEM

ENHANCE CATFULNESS. Imagine you're a cat and take a step back. Look at your current situation from a position of safety and relax. Note what you see without engaging the emotions and find your zen.

_____

_____

_____

_____

_____

_____

_____

_____

_____

_____

_____

_____

_____

_____

_____

_____

_____

_____

'I HAVE LIVED WITH
SEVERAL ZEN MASTERS
– ALL OF THEM CATS.'

ECKHART TOLLE

'AFTER
DARK ALL
CATS ARE
LEOPARDS.'

ZUNI PROVERB

THE ART OF SQUEEZING INTO SMALL SPACES. Be flexible like our feline friends. If there isn't a way through a problem find a way around it, be cat and go the extra mile.

'A CAT,
I AM SURE,
COULD WALK ON A
CLOUD
WITHOUT COMING
THROUGH.'

JULES VERNE

STORYBOARD IT OUT

Outline your problem using pictures and words until you get stuck. If this were a story, how would you like it to end? Write down the steps you can take to reach the best solution.

LIFE IS
BETTER WITH
cat naps

WORK WITH
YOUR DREAMS

Before you take a cat nap, reflect on what you want in the future that could help you in your life now...

When you wake, note down:

Images, symbols and narratives that you recall:

_____

_____

_____

_____

_____

_____

_____

_____

_____

_____

How you feel, and any strong emotions from
your dream:

_____

_____

_____

_____

_____

_____

_____

What do you think your dream is telling
you about your current situation?

_____

_____

_____

_____

_____

_____

_____

TRUST THE *whiskers,* THEY NEVER LIE!

THE POWER OF SLEEP. Catch a quality cat nap. Switch off all electrical devices at least an hour before bed.

'WAY DOWN DEEP, WE'RE ALL MOTIVATED BY THE SAME URGES. CATS HAVE THE COURAGE TO LIVE BY THEM.'

JIM DAVIS

GO WILD. Be a free spirit and do what you want to do, not what others expect of you.

SHAKE THINGS UP

Make a note of three small changes you can make to your usual routine which will take you out of your comfort zone. Little things, such as taking a different route to work or trying lunch somewhere new.

Cats seek out adventure and so can you!

1. Going on a daily walk or bike ride, and exploring different parts of the neighborhood.

2.

3.

STRETCH IT OUT

Make two lists, one of your current sleep habits and the other of things that would improve your night's rest.

Cross out any habits you'd like to eliminate from the first list and underline those you'd like to practise from the second, then introduce them into your usual routine.

'I HAVE STUDIED MANY PHILOSOPHERS AND MANY CATS. THE WISDOM OF CATS IS INFINITELY SUPERIOR.'

HIPPOLYTE TAINE

CATTED DETERMINATION. The ever-determined kitty draws on its resolve when lesser mortals might throw in the towel. Be resilient and always believe in your dreams.

I CAT AND I WILL!

'I Cat!' is the top kitty mantra. Make it part of your vocabulary. This will help you develop an open-minded, 'Cat Do' attitude in all aspects of your life.

Start a sentence 'I Cat...' and come up with three new things you can do this year that you've never tried before.

I CAT...

_____

_____

_____

_____

_____

_____

_____

I CAT...

I CAT...

UNLEASH
YOUR
purr

'THE PROBLEM WITH CATS IS THAT THEY GET THE SAME EXACT LOOK WHETHER THEY SEE A MOTH OR AN AXE-MURDERER.'

PAULA POUNDSTONE

FELINE FLOW. Don't set boundaries, instead take a step back without judgement and let things unfold. Give yourself time to assess the situation before reacting.

FIND YOUR
inner
MEOW

REFOCUS. Ever noticed how a cat can spend hours staring into space? Sometimes you need to switch off to rejuvenate the senses before trying again. Whether an errant butterfly catches your attention or a tempting morsel from the fridge, let the distraction lift your spirits!

'A CAT CAN BE
TRUSTED
TO PURR
WHEN SHE IS PLEASED,
WHICH IS MORE THAN
CAN BE SAID FOR
HUMAN BEINGS.'

WILLIAM RALPH INGE

TAKE A BREATHER. Focus on your breathing, making inward breaths deeper and outward breaths longer. Rather than worrying or forcing thoughts, just take notice of what you see and feel and let it pass through you and out of the top of your head.

YOU DON'T HAVE TO BE *perfect* TO BE *amazing*

WALK ON THE WILD SIDE

Cats leap with wild abandonment and a positive
approach to life is vital to success. Make a note
of your short-term goals and ambitions and think
about the leaps you can make to achieve them.

'I LOVE CATS
BECAUSE I ENJOY
MY HOME; AND
LITTLE BY LITTLE,
THEY BECOME ITS
VISIBLE SOUL.'

JEAN COCTEAU

'CATS SLEEP ANYWHERE, ANY TABLE, ANY CHAIR, TOP OF PIANO, WINDOW-LEDGE, IN THE MIDDLE, ON THE EDGE, OPEN DRAWER, EMPTY SHOE, ANYBODY'S LAP WILL DO.'

ELEANOR FARJEON

LIVE LESS OUT OF *habit* AND MORE OUT OF *intent*

'IN ANCIENT
TIMES CATS WERE
WORSHIPPED
AS GODS;
THEY HAVE NOT
FORGOTTEN THIS.'

TERRY PRATCHETT

BE KIND TO YOURSELF. Cats understand the need to enjoy life. They do what they need to do to be a happy kitty. Indulge in a pampering session, or treat yourself simply because you're wonderful!

LIVE IN THE MOMENT

Cats appreciate everything from the breeze on their face to the piece of fluff they find to play with behind the sofa.

Take five minutes every day to appreciate what you have. Note down five things you're grateful for and why.

1.
_____
_____
_____
_____
_____

2.
_____
_____
_____
_____
_____

3.

4.

5.

MAKE
cattitude
YOUR
attitude